AF494943

PRAXIS

πρᾶξις

Editions.Hunter

ISBN 978-2-9546285-0-9

For Eli.

With illustrations by Carla Adol.

PRAXIS

praxis (πρᾶξις) – activity engaged in by free people.

Foreword

I have often attempted to formulate this philosophy which I name 'Praxis'.

Hesitation has often gotten the better of me as in reality, all of the wisdom of the world exists in written form already.

What use then is another work on a subject which is, in my judgement, long solved and understood?

The problem which exists in our age is perhaps that we have too much information and no fixed method or structure within which to understand the information which is presented to us, so that with our limited time, it becomes more and more difficult to get to the meaning of things, and we end up with a confusion of ideas.

Even if some of these ideas are essentially useful, they become difficult to use in our lives.

Understanding the mind is a craft in itself, and in my view, the highest craft there is.

My fundamental understanding is that behind all words lies meaning, and that this meaning is universal and timeless, so that, whatever has been understood in the past and represented in whatever language and in whatever cultural context, the meaning or 'essence' remains the same.

Acknowledgements

I would like to thank Mr Arnold, author and systems-analyst, who took me under his wing as an informal tutor and friend while I was studying at Bedales School.
I will never forget him nor the impact he has had on my life through his incredible insight.

Summer Govan and Christopher Hamilton, my former philosophy teachers at Bedales provided me with the foundations of the discipline and were always kind and encouraging towards me, for this I thank them without measure.

I would equally like to thank my family for their understanding and patience, without them and their support this work would never have materialised.

My appreciation also goes to the late Will Durant, author of the epic 'Story of Civilization' which gives great insight into the nature of human affairs over time.

Don't fear god,
Don't worry about death;
What is good is easy to get, and
What is terrible is easy to endure
(Philodemus, Herculaneum *Papyrus, 1005, 4.9–14*).

Ἄφοβον ὁ θεός,
ἀνύποπτον ὁ θάνατος
καὶ τἀγαθὸν μὲν εὔκτητον,
τὸ δὲ δεινὸν εὐεκκαρτέρητον
(Philodemus, Herculaneum *Papyrus, 1005, 4.9–14*)

What I write here then, is merely an attempt through common symbols with heavily shifting foundations to communicate to your internal sense of meaning.

This is a concise book or 'distillation' of philosophy which has as its primary objective to aid the reader in understanding what I consider to be the meaning of existence, explained as simply as possible.

It is not particularly complicated to read, nor to understand, but requires awareness and reflection and the removal of prejudice.

The most difficult part of 'Praxis' is to live it, to include it in one's life at all moments, no matter what situation one finds oneself in.

This work is divided into axioms, upon which propositions are derived. The axioms explain 'why' things are the way they are, the propositions explain 'how' we reach this understanding and apply it to our lives.

There will also be examples given where I have deemed it appropriate.

Each page, illustration & diagram must be considered *lento gradu,* so that their meaning may be fully absorbed. Although a short book, this is the fruit of many years of reflection, study and stands upon the shoulders of many great thinkers.

Many passages have a Greek translation of the essential idea being represented. Although it is unnecessary to read these translations it will provide a greater insight to the reader if they wish to read more philosophy in the future.

Our lives are shadows. Our essence we understand only from the perspective of infinity.

A1. The universe is infinite (Apeiron ἄπειρον).

The universe is infinite and comprised of a single substance which can be perceived by man as two distinct *modes*: *thought* and *extension*.

When one considers the universe as essentially infinite and constant there is no change and therefore no form, in this sense the universe is 'formless'.

We perceive this formless nature of the universe when we cease to separate ourselves into individual ego's with associated id's and consider ourselves as being seamless parts of the universal whole.

A2. The essence of man is *desire* or *will.*

This *desire* moves through the modes as clear and distinct or intuitive *understanding* or as *passion* or *affection.*

Once a *passion* is understood it becomes an *affection* which is then possibly moderated with virtue.

No matter what your circumstances or mental state, this knowledge is essential, as the universe encompasses all *thought* and *extension.*

It is the totality of all true understanding & positive emotion as well as all matter.

Negative emotion, as destruction, cannot be considered as a 'thing' but as the absence of positivity and construction.

Knowing this one is able to turn oneself towards this essential all enveloping substance and find peace and friendship with oneself and with the universe (Apatheia ἀπάθεια) .

A3. All forms (Morphe μορφη) change.

Thoughts are constantly being moved by desire as are bodies, when considered within the perspective of infinity, all combinations of all bodies and thoughts must occur, it is for this reason that we perceive such things as good and bad, when in fact we would be better advised to perceive them all as *necessary occurrences.* In the same way that objects must fall due to gravitational forces.

Once we understand that human affairs and individual human beings move as do the seasons in nature we understand the cyclical character of form.
One thing cannot live eternally unless it be infinite and the only thing which is infinite is the formless universal substance (Hypokeimenon ὑποκείμενον).

A4. Time does not exist in infinity.

As the universe has no beginning nor end, one's conception of time becomes meaningless as there is no movement (Atopy ἀτοπία) from this perspective.

We speak of the *passing of time* which gives a true indication as to what we mean by time, that of the division of movement into moments.

All actions are conditionally determined and fall within a pattern, which will ultimately occur when viewed from the perspective of infinity.

As no line is truly straight and as all bend in the Riemannian sense, all vectors follow spherical infinite paths, one cannot perceive a 'moment' in time as there is no such point, and no possible measurement to quantify it.

When viewed from the perspective of the infinite, form does not exist, and without form there is no movement and without movement there is no time.

Therefore time does not exist.

Left. I Ching Trigram representing 'The Creative' Right. Combinatorial Directed Graph representing the same concept N=4.

A5. Freedom is understanding (Hexis ἕξις).

One's freedom is found simply in the understanding of oneself and the universe in which one exists (Henosis ἕνωσις).

In the exercise of our faculties using the optimum method to understand this idea.

By doing so we free ourselves more and more from the servitude of attachment.

All unclear 'confused' ideas are the cause of our mental suffering & the more we perceive the self and the universe as they really exist the closer we come to freedom. The most interesting phenomenon which will occur to anyone who is mentally 'active' is that their internal energy will move as it were 'up the spine' from the basis of sexual desire (eros Ἔρως) upwards to the stomach and onwards to the higher emotional attachments and the aesthetic and finally towards clear and distinct understanding.

Once one has entered into the development of clear and distinct ideas there is a disconnection between these lesser forms of desire and this state of understanding.

One will inevitably fall backwards once one has reached a certain level of understanding (**Bathos βάθος**) and the desires (Eros Ἔρως) will naturally return. But with greater virtue, the overall ability of the mind to control desire and discipline it through moderation (Arete ἀρετή) will to some extent eliminate the degree to which physical desires would otherwise impede the mental development of the self.

What is important is to take the first step, to remain aware and to try.

A6. The purpose of existence is to seek inner contentment (Eudaimonia εὐδαιμονία) with the absence of pain (Aponia ἀπονία).

The fundamental meaning of life is to be found in a sense of inner contentment which lasts indefinitely.

No higher feeling can be found than this.

It appears to me self-evident that if one were able to maintain a constant state of inner contentment one would logically not require another purpose in life.

One may say that inner contentment is nothing more than obtaining that which one desires. But this would be false, as inner contentment requires that one no longer needs that which one would have otherwise

desired.
To remove all desire is again, not something which might be understood as repression of desire but the transference of this desire towards other ends.

It is certain that the body requires certain things, that without these things the body will become diseased and die, but this should not be seen as a cause of mental suffering as the body will eventually change form and die anyway.

The inevitability of life is in itself a cause for Eudaimonia.

There is no urgency in life if one is unafraid of death. This feeling that one may take one's time is essential when attempting to maintain a sense of inner peace.

No opinion (Doxa δόξα), *no judgement made against you, nor honour bestowed or withheld, no wealth nor power, will affect the person who is interested in their inner contentment above all.*

If your intentions are for all to find peace, all negative views must be ignored. It is critical that behind peace, there is force, and a force which is greater than the negative force.

A7. One cannot understand by the cumulation of sense-impressions alone.

In order to understand meanings one must analyse sense-impressions & intentions. If I have a noun such as ball I may associate this with a spherical object.

But this information does not explain anything but the essence of the word ball.

Equally if I included a subject and a verb and perhaps an adjective:

'The girl kicked the ball.' this still provides only partial information.

What is now required is an explanation of the 'intentions' of the subject in performing this action:

'The girl kicked the ball because she wanted to win the game.'

In this sentence we understand not only the stages involved but also the intentions of the subject in question.

This surpasses the cumulation of sense-impressions and reaches into the analysis of intentions and thus meaning.

The left line represents extension, the right, thought. When one interprets thought as an attribute of extension one creates a 'belief' (radical materialism).

This can be inverted to signify a system of thought which attributes everything to thought and nothing to extension (radical idealism).

In reality both thought and extension exist in parallel and ultimately together as one reality.

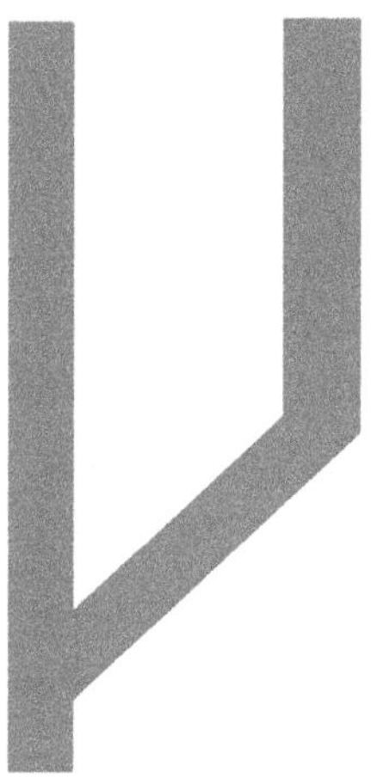

A8. Our understanding is limited to our reason (Prohairesis προαίρεσις) alone.

Once we have moved beyond the interpretation of the world via external perception alone we extract from this 'patterns', these patterns are the ways in which we understand the structure of our selves and the universe.

In the same way that one understands the idea of the sphere without requiring one to be present.

We can divide up these states as:

Relative Subjectivity – Where the self considers the self alone as an emotional subject and does not consider anything else.
Relative Objectivity – Where the self considers everything as objects including the

self.

Objectivity – Where the self consider the sum total (in principle) of all extension and thought.

Subjectivity – Where the self considers the interrelation of emotional subjects.

A9. The universe and all within it is never random, even if it acts without finality.

The universe is then constructed by 'laws' which are simply geometric 'limits' imposed by the internal logic of the universe. There can be no 'chance' in such a universe, which is determined to act in the way that it does.

Man often interprets the world around him in terms of *chance*, but this is simply the realisation that events do not always repeat in a way which is always predictable to oneself.

If one were to spin a roulette wheel, by the physical properties involved, all events that will occur over time in front of the spectator would have no doubt attached to them.

The fact that the spectator does not possess this information does not mean that the universe is ignorant of the outcome.

One may wish to consider the nature of *chance* as an infinite series of prime numbers, unique in its composition.

Prime Number Identification Algorithm

$$\mathbf{2\text{^}((p-1)-1)/p}$$

If sum is a whole number - prime

If sum is a fraction - non-prime

A10. One cannot understand through belief.

One may read something and agree because of a preconditioned idea as to its 'truth' but this is nothing more than a belief.

To know something, it must be understood.

A good example of this would be that I believe 2 x 9 = 18 because I remember having been taught this equation, however, I only know that this is the answer when I think of the number 9 and add an additional 9, this then relies on my understanding of what makes up the number 9 which is essentially 9 x 1 and so on.

Only when one has broken apart a belief into its individual units is it possible to say that one understands a thing in itself.

A11. Intuition (Nous νόος) is the supreme method of understanding.

Intuition is equivalent to one knowing that there is a short-cut in a maze, that it is unnecessary to carry out every single operation or walk every single path to find what one is looking for. Some people need to walk around the maze, some spend their entire lives in it, and some quickly move through and find the exit.

When viewed on the diagram (Annex 2) it would signify a short-cut AEF...A.

G1. Belief is essential to the majority and to governing men.

Although one cannot act reasonably through belief, the majority of people will do so. If there were no such mechanism for controlling the populace there one would rely solely on positive and negative conditioning (the threat of force and the promise of reward) when these are enforced or the general perception is that they will be enforced (belief) this will be an effective if overly complex method of control however when unenforced will create anarchy, then a reformulated power in the same way that ice melts when heated and reforms when cooled.

When the population is directed towards a belief structure & when the leadership has good intentions which *emulate via the use of emotions* (Pathos πάθος) the Ethos (ἦθος) of the group to have the Demos exercise truth without *explaining* it as such (Logos) the population will be at peace and in security within that society.

G2. Politics and therefore the control of *extension (Polis πόλις)* is based on authority *auctoritas (belief)* and power *potestas (force)*.

This power is in turn derived by universal laws. If it is abused it is broken down and then built up again as light is swallowed in a vacuum.

The ontology of power is rule by one, by the few and by many. One can perceive the cyclical motion of these political systems as triangles expanding and collapsing like a house of cards.

Power is necessary, as is its concentration, no group of people will remain in a state of anarchy, as power will naturally organise all elements in a given political subsystem (Humanitas). Essentially, order will always prevail.

With the increasing understanding of the applied sciences, technology has enabled political agents to extend their control over *extension* which is still, it must be mentioned, permitted only within the laws of the universe.

PRAXIS

Given what has been mentioned above, one would if so persuaded wish to understand not simply *why* one would wish to achieve a state of perpetual inner contentment but to understand *how* one would begin to go about doing this.

P1. Praxis is a conscious awareness of one's emotional and physical state (thought /extension).

One is only ready to take the first step when one is in doubt (Epoche ἐποχή), when one is uncertain and is looking to learn more about one's self and about that which encompasses reality in its totality (Khôra χώρα).

There can be no certainty unless one has already doubted everything which one believes.

When one is uncertain as Lao Tzu once said it is as if ones thoughts were like grains of sand in a glass of water, it is necessary to be patient so that all the grains sink to the bottom thus enabling one to see through the water clearly.

P2. The opposite of Praxis is a passive state of dependency on one's desire.

This desire concentrates in many emotional and physical states of which one is ignorant of the origin and unable to change (Aporia ἀπορία).

By reducing the self into extension and placing thought within this, one is actually causing a great internal imbalance, the consequence of this imbalance are a total lack of self understanding, a relative objectification of the self and of others and the reduction of the emotions to the bodily functions of pleasure and pain. This does not mean that negative and positive emotional responses will not occur, but it means that all responses will be tightly defined by the external world, and that the self considering this to be the case will be governed or will conspire to govern everything as much as possible, in order to influence this environment for its own interests. The self will also attribute emotional responses with physical causes.

There can be no inner contentment when the self views things with such a lack of clarity..

When viewed in terms of the diagram (Annex A) one understands this state as being simply treating means as ends. When one should always consider the ends as being separate from the means.

P3. With this awareness one is able to analyse the changes which occur in these two aspects of self.

In order to develop this awareness one must be in a quiet environment where all the emotions which are in flux can be observed clearly.

Pay attention (Hypomnema ὑπόμνημα) to all underlying reasons behind the emotions that are being experienced.

The fluctuations of the self will become more apparent the more one is aware of one's self.

The fluctuations are between a negative state and a positive state which will in the passive state of dependency be entirely dictated by the external forms but over time will become reigned.

The calculus of emotional states.

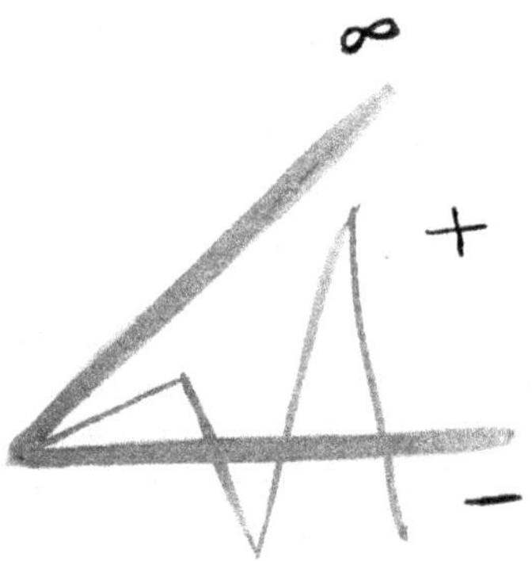

In the above diagram one may understand the fluctuating line as emotional flux from a sense of joy to a sense of sadness one ultimately relying on another.
The diagonal line signifies understanding requiring no attachment to external objects is constant and increments the more one understands.

Knowledge is then, not understanding, for understanding requires correct intentions as well as knowledge of their correct application.

It is important that one does not attempt to 'block' an emotion, for this is not understanding, instead, observe it (Hypomnema ὑπόμνημα) and consider how this emotion fits with one's objectives (Telos τέλος).

The body is often a useful place to start when understanding this concept. If one is immodest in food or alcohol, poisons the body with drugs or expends all effort through the pursuit of money, fame or the love of power, it is clear that these will be the main targets for one's analysis. One must ask oneself, if this pursuit is driven by the self or if the self is being driven by a desire

which one is seemingly unable to control.
It is however highly reasonable to perform these changes slowly.

More important are the subtle changes which occur vis a vis our affections which we may consider to be good when they are in fact causing us harm.
Consider the concept of justice, if one were to perceive that the action of another was unjust, one may feel a sense of indignation, but this emotion is a negative response. This does not mean that one should not discriminate between the just (Dike Dicé) and the unjust, even if there are many degrees of relativity between the two, but it means that regardless of one's judgement as to the justice of an action one must never respond with anything other than a sense of internal joy and understanding, to put it precisely, that all that exists in form is a

fluctuating movement of actions and that within form there will always be many combinations of events, that perfection is the combination of all possible events in form. When this is understood one can view all events as being *necessary.*

P4. Once analysed one is able to identify the aspects of one's self which are causing the most harm.

Some of these areas will be easily addressed, others will be much more difficult and may require more time. If an area is particularly difficult to remove, moderation should be applied. Extremism in suppressing an emotional response will not stop that response, but simply suppress it causing it to resurface in the future with greater intensity. It is only when one has understood that this emotional response is not 'necessary' that it will dissipate over time and become replaced with a 'necessary' response. One cannot surround one's internal mental environment with negativity and expect positive understanding to be constant, it will instead fluctuate.

P5. Virtue is the consequence of praxis.

By being aware (Daimon δαίμων), by identifying the fluctuations of self and the individual areas which need to be addressed to reduce harm, one is able to apply virtue, meaning a power over the self, where joy and reason meet.

What is this emotion which we speak of? It is a physical reaction, but a physical reaction which coincides with a mental thought process, both co-exist, and subsequently when we speak of joy and reason, we mean the physical and mental co-incidence of a heightened sense of understanding.

P6. Virtue (Ataraxia ἀταραξία) protects the self against negative attachments.

False joy (Hedone Ἡδονή) which comes from attachment requires the presence of external things and the associated negative components of joy affect the self to a lesser extent over time and are replaced with genuine internal joy (Eudaimonia εὐδαιμονία) *which projects outwards and is in no way reliant on external conditions.*

Many of us are exposed to a culture which stresses the importance of money, sexual attractiveness, power and honour. These are however means and not ends (Adiaphora ἀδιάφορα), *if one were to treat these things as ends one would corrupt oneself and move away from a balanced emotional state.*

When treated as means, they are however, quite appropriate in order to further the self as well as the common good.

It is perhaps a side effect of modern secularism that instead of separating church and state the state has developed a *theology of materialism* which currently prevails among the 'leading' states, and will in time be replaced, if for no other reason than that it is causing a tremendous degree of social instability.

P7. Virtue aids others in finding their own joy and reason through conscious awareness.

Because the self distinguishes less and less the forms of things one removes all distinctions between the self and the external world (Dyad dýo), the inner self projects outwards in a virtuous stream removing all negativity and harm and replacing it with joy.

Whenever one is confronted with a feeling of sadness, be it hatred, jealousy or any other negative emotion towards an external object one must simply let go of that object, as it is the self which suffers from this feeling, the object is not the 'cause' of this negative response.

One must respond to a negative person by

leading them towards virtue, by expressing joy and friendship from one's self and in so doing one will become stronger and will weaken the negativity in the other person at the same time.

Equally if one comes across a person who has an entirely negative feeling towards oneself one may forgive him as it is his emotional reaction which is at cause and not one's behaviour.

P8. Power is understanding of the self.

By understanding the self one can truly speak of power, when speaking of power as the ability to control others or one's external environment this would only be true if the self were using this external control for the betterment of the common good, if however this power was simply an external manifestation of an internal love of power, or, feeling of superiority over others (Thumos θυμός) or the external environment this would be an unbalanced emotional state and would in fact describe somebody who is lacking in internal, true power (Akrasia ἀκρασία).

Instead of using one's own force against someone who is ignorant, one must, if unable to avoid him, to use the force of his opponent in order to correct him or punish him so that this behaviour is not repeated.

P9. Dreams are the mental representations of emotional states.

As the mind is less attentive when sleeping, the images which represent the ideas in the self are placed in sequences. This is an attempt by the mind to create a sense of order, to explain a situation or a problem, so that a resolution may be struck later on. The mind does not require a literal representation of an idea, and will piece together whatever images or other sensory information which correspond with the emotion which is being analysed. When interpreting a dream it is therefore essential to analyse the emotion that was present and not simply the images present.

P10. The self when considered in infinity is infinite.

When one realises for a moment the immanent nature of the universe one is in union (Henosis ἕνωσις) with the universe.

It is a consequence of this mental appreciation that the self will feel its proper place relative to the universe, that all goodness belongs to the universe and is not to be monopolised by the self, this feeling can be shared infinitely and cannot be limited by someone else's understanding of the same concept.

A déjà vu is an equivalent and common emotion, when one 'feels' that an event is repeating.

In reality it is a moment when the self

perceives infinity in which all moments have their origin.

T1.Without physical health, the mind will begin to fail.

It may appear to the reader, to be self evident, that without exercise & correct diet one's health will be effective. The optimal form of healthcare is prevention, as, once a problem materialises, it will be more difficult to remedy.

T2. Without organisation of time we will not be able to complete our objectives.

Whether it be conscious or unconscious we must manage our time effectively.

The simplest way to do this, is to reflect on what we spend our time doing and see if there is anything which is working *against our development* and if there is any *possibility of changing* this.

The waking day is divided up into a series of sequences which we perform by habit or necessity, these must all be broken down and analysed to see if they are truly necessary and if so, whether they can be improved upon.

Footnote

The metaphysics, ethics, logic & epistemology of Praxis agree with all philosophies and philosophical systems upon which I have deliberated, these being: Ethica of Benedictus de Spinoza, The Combinatorial Method of A. Arnold (of which a combinatorial directed graph is included in this work), the early Taoist texts such as the first book of the I Ching & the poetry of the Tao Te Ching, as well as some elements of Stoicism as practised by the ancient Greeks.

I would encourage the reader to consider as I have these various philosophies and in so doing to appreciate the similarities between them to come perhaps to my initial estimation, that meaning underlies everything and that truth is universal.

Glossary

Substance – The sum total of all thought and extension.

Mode – A division of Substance

Thought – A succession of distinct ideas.

Extension – A succession of distinct actions.

Affection – An emotion with the idea of an external cause.

Passion – An emotion with the idea of an external cause which is not perceived by the self.

Desire – The essence of man.

Clockwise from the top, starting from the outside working in, with three levels within each 'leaf'.

Serenity, Joy, Ecstasy, Acceptance, Trust, Admiration, Apprehension, Fear, Terror, Distraction, Surprise, Amazement, Pensiveness, Sadness, Grief, Boredom, Disgust, Loathing, Annoyance, Anger, Rage, Interest, Anticipation, Vigilance.

Annex of the Combinatorial System

Mr Arnold's Combinatorial System as applied to Psychology. Below is an N=6 (6 factors) Directed Graph.

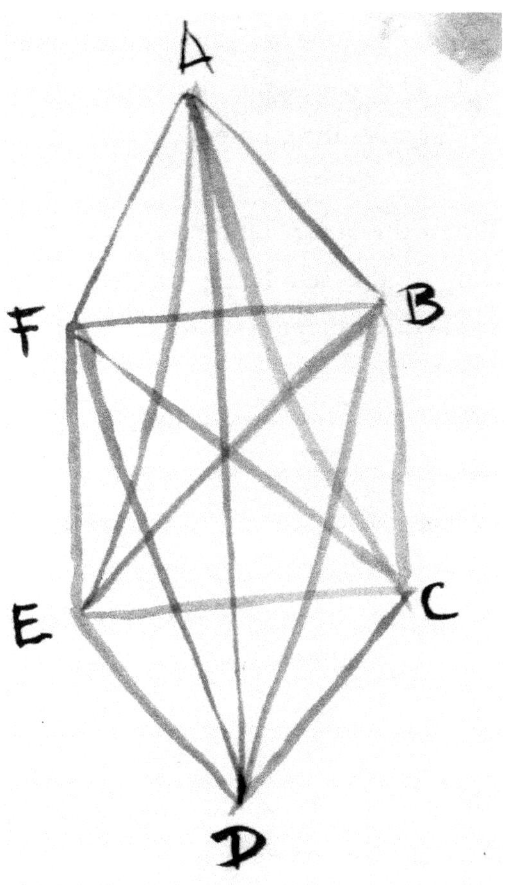
A
B
F
C
E
D

A – Signifies the Self (intention or cause)
B, C, D & E – Signify the Stages (how)
F – Signifies the Consequence

When the arrow terminates at F this is akin to the self being trapped in the world of sense impressions.

When the arrow returns from F to A this signifies a state of learning and understanding.

When the arrow reaches F but feeds back to another Stage, this is akin to a belief.

When the arrow terminates before reaching the consequence and is instead blocked at a Stage, this indicates that something is obstructing one's progress.

It should also be noted that in one graph it is possible to perceive multiple different outcomes depending on the options chosen, one may feasibly conceive of a graph which has one sequence feeding back to the self, another terminating at the consequence and another feeding back to a stage. It is this that individuals interpret as randomness, as it is possible that one may learn something when the intention was simply to treat that learning situation as a means to an end.

Contents

www.ingramcontent.com/pod-product-compliance
Ingram Content Group UK Ltd.
Pitfield, Milton Keynes, MK11 3LW, UK
UKHW021642190726
13853UKWH00001B/5

9 782954 628509